THE INCREDIBLE GIFT OF SCHIZOPHRENIA SIGHED THE HOST

THE INCREDIBLE GIFT OF SCHIZOPHRENIA SIGHED THE HOST

Goose Punk

Copyright © 2018 by Goose Punk.

ISBN: Softcover   978-1-9845-5846-6
               eBook   978-1-9845-5845-9

All rights reserved. No part of this book may be reproduced or transmitted in any form or by any means, electronic or mechanical, including photocopying, recording, or by any information storage and retrieval system, without permission in writing from the copyright owner.

The views expressed in this work are solely those of the author and do not necessarily reflect the views of the publisher, and the publisher hereby disclaims any responsibility for them.

Any people depicted in stock imagery provided by Getty Images are models, and such images are being used for illustrative purposes only. Certain stock imagery © Getty Images.

Print information available on the last page.

Rev. date: 10/08/2018

To order additional copies of this book, contact:
Xlibris
1-888-795-4274
www.Xlibris.com
Orders@Xlibris.com
786287

Korea's nuclear program looks like the launching of the space shuttle. Could it be that's what they think they're doing? Could it be North Korea saw the launching of the space shuttle, & remembers the end of WW2. So they've devised a nuclear bomb strapped to a rocket just like we did?

CHAPTER 1

THERE WERE TWO cops in this town whome I knew there faces. One's name was Lou I believe, & the other one has gone blind after being shot in the head. The rest of them are like clones. Straight out of the cookie cutter. The rest you might say, are Nottingham soldiers. History repeats itself. Now, Putin was self appointed. We know this, the President of Russia currently put himself in power. Trump, our current President, may have done the same thing in cahoots with Russia. It's been all over the news for the last year & a half that Russia may have had something to do with Trumps winning the election. Who's to say that Russia didn't help Trump help himself to President of the USA. Now, I don't know if your familiar with The Story of Robin Hood, but in that story, there was the good King Richard, & there was his lazy brother The Sherrif. While Richard was away, The Sherrif of Nottingham seized power in England. He was trying to smuggle valubles from London to Nottingham where Robin's Merry Men intercepted the jewels. Does anybody see what I see here? The likeness between the scrawney lion on the Disney version of Robin Hood, & Little John & Trump laying around The White House, Tweeting detramental, & hatefull things towards the people of the USA? I think Trump is dangerous in The White House as far as forighn relations. When he says now on his trip to North Korea, "We might be leaving in a hurry". That just means there's a threat that North Korea might not welcome the west & there could be an all out war because of what Trump is trying to achieve. But what is Trump trying to achieve? He is already supposed to be one of the richest people in the entire world. Why would he need to pull off this entire scam? I don't see him needing any more money, unless he isn't so rich anymore. I he says they might be leaving North Korea in a hurry, it sounds like somebody's advice. Putins advice maybe? Putin & Trump seem to be talking quite a bit. In kahoots you might say. Now, where would the need for money come from, Russia probably.

CHAPTER 2

IT'S LIKE HALIBURTON, the government hires a private army to do the so called fighting so they don't need congress to declare war. They can go to war anytime they like. The same thing happened to the police dept. in our town. They call it a "Police Agency" now. They privatized the liquor industry so you have to buy your liquor in public at the supermarket, & you can't do a little drinking at home at night without all the people who are shopping with their kids seeing you buy it. For this reason I believe that's why my own mother drank till the day she died. Because, all is lost she's a public drunk, & if she tried to quit, & relapsed, boom she's back in AA because all those fools talk, talk, talk. Getting fucked up is always kept on the downlow, & done discretly. This is what you call a form of prohibition. It ain't right & it never will be. Marijuana too, it's legal in our state. Though they are still doing illigal marijuana busts. If they can't tax it, you can't smoke it. I don't see them privatizing the marijuana stores anytime soon though because, it would make pot sales way too convinient. Right now, the young people who want pot have to go to the outskirts of town to get to the pot shops. Putting it in the grocery stores would make it way to easy for them to buy. At anytime the felt they needed it they could just walk into a store, & since the stigma isn't so high on pot, it'd be a positive on drug use.

CHAPTER 3

MY DAD & I were invited to a Mininite dinner once. We were picked up on the farm by one of them, & dropped off after dinner. While at dinner, everybody prayed before they ate. After the prayre, my dad leaned over the table & said, "My son & I aren't the most religious people". Everybody ate, then we were driven home. When we got out of the car, my dad said to me, "They make their kids quit school in the eigth grade so that they can control their women better". Now, we know that The NRA is fundamentally Christian. So, does that mean that possibly Religious Right is who are behind all these school shootings in the last 20 years. I think they might be too because, if they can keep the children from learning in school, this premotes the idea that they can control their women better. We went to this dinner in Canada where quitting school might not be such an issue, but in America if you can achieve this on a large scale you can seriously impact the way things are going by keeping the youth dumb & controling their minds with bible construments.

CHAPTER 4

WHAT'S THE SHERRIF imbesling? Well in our town, there is an increaced amount of trains running through the city every day. For the last few years, somebody's been shipping coal & oil by way of railway, day after day after day. If you look real close at some of the older oil cars, they read, "liquid petrolium gas". I looked up liquid petrolium gas on the internet, & it's used in heating homes. It's not oil at all like their protest signs read, but something else. My old Elementary school is actually being shut down, & they're actually building a new school. I read in the paper a few years ago that the coal trains were shaking the students in the school so bad they were actually considering moving the school. Looks like they're really gonna do it. Isn't that unbelievable? 25 years ago in this town, there was only one or two trains a day. At night we used to sleep out on the lawn, & wait for the train to pass every night at midnight. The train was actually concientious enough to come through at midnight back then. What's happening now?

CHAPTER 5

(L ET'S IMAGINE) THEY say there's a lot of 'what if's', but what if Trump, while putting all these tarrifs on China is actually mistaken like Columbus was? Say he thinks he's tarrifing China while he's actually persecuting some unknown land where the people think he'd descended from the sky, & his financers want new Christian souls, & gold from these people who aren't black, or white. Well, it's fun to loose & to pretend Mr. Trump. "Everything seems like we're in India, but it ain't quite right", said Trump in a recent interview on Fox. These people aren't liking our worthless beads, & are trembling in fear. They offer us wonderous gifts, but there isn't any gold, tea, or silk. These pricless items must be extracted from these people whether obvious or not, the existence of what we want is aperently hidden, & we will not be stopped until we have what we want.

CHAPTER 6

PEOPLE PROTESTING GUN violence now in 2018 out number the sea of old geezers who supported Trump after the 2016 election while demonstrating at The Capital. These students will be of age to vote, & are planning to register to vote & edjucate accordingly so nothing like this Trumpingham happens again. These are young people who are tired of fearing going to school, & do not want teachers armed in defense against school shooters. I compliment them on their devotion, as I'm against firearms, & having lost my gun rights several times due to being commited for mental illness, I've not missed not having my gun rights, & think these trigger happy white supremacists need to lose their gun rights so it might make them all think. While against war & government for the most part, I do believe in now terms it's nescissary to have military with the current government status, but strictly voulantary. Having never wanted to join. I also believe the military are the only people in America who need to have any guns. It's wrong to have them to hunt these days with extiction such a widespread problem, & home protection would be a lot less of a nescessity if the robbers were without weopons aswell. Now, without a Federal Government nor any state government, it might be more nescissary for a normal citizen to want a weopon as China could march over The Berring Strait, & we just might need to militantly defend our property, but at this current moment such a threat does not exist.

CHAPTER 7

I N AN IDEAL democracy, majority rules. In ours however as we know there's a series of electoral colleges. Canada is a true democracy where the leaders can be voted out at any given time. In America, we have to suffer through the lame ducks, & that's why it's so painstaking to be an American, the government. America is supposed to be run by the people, & if these young people now getting of age to vote do, they can change the country toward a more positive future if the votes voted are counted coodingly with the electoral college. Like, as long as they win enough states to add up. Not everyone in California, but nobody in any of the states in the bible belt. This means we gotta move off the coast, & get in there, mess with Texas, & show those geezers what were about, & get back out of the big cities. The young people can do it, & I for one want them to. I think most people in the country have their opinions in the right place, but I also believe Trumpingham, & the assholes in power have a stronghold on the electoral colleges, & statigicaly win elections by stratigically placing votes. This will make them hard to beat, & hard to remove from power. In 2008 when we elected Obama, Europe was amazed that we were able to completly overthrow the government without firing a single shot. Obama turned out to be a flake, but that's beside the point. We still completely changed the government from Republican to Democrat with one critical election. Now is the time to remove these grey haired so & so's from power, & now, the young people out number the old, & we can do it if we stay strong, & vote.

CHAPTER 8

T EACHERS CARRYING WEOPONS is a bad idea too. It's simply setting a bad example for the kids in class. "The teacher carries a gun, why can't I?" & so on & so forth. You have to set a good example as an adult, & for most kids their teacher spends just as much time with them as their working parents, so if the teacher is setting a bad example, & mom & dad have guns at home, what's to stop the kid from packing? "Gun free classes, & a gun free world." is what the young people are saying & it's time we listened to our kids because, in my home I was to be seen & not heard when I was little, & I was kicked around like the silent nose picker I was. I wasn't listened to, & I wasn't respected as someone who was capable of thinking for myself till I got older, & these kids now, need to be listened to because, their classmates are dying, & being ignored in the same fashion as the way Trump denies the existence of global warming. The cowardly lion he is.

CHAPTER 9

IT'S BEEN SAID that the way Trump stole the election in 2016 was he took peoples names that were common like Smith, or Gonzolez, & made it so all Jake McCoys were erased from the ballots except one. Without the voters actually knowing they were erased. So, all the people with a common name were reduced to only one vote. It's called a cross check. In turn, The Russians might not have influenced the election at all. Unless it was their idea. And, I do see evidence of Trump being led by somebody else when he says, "We might be leaving very quickly" when talking about his visit to North Korea.

CHAPTER 10

HERE'S A THOUGHT on the actual meaning of 'disability'. If I want to disable the wifi on my computer, I simply have to open the right window, & turn it off. It doesn't origionally come that way, but if I want it disabled I, the operator can turn it off, & use my computer for other things without wifi. I was a normal kid with an overactive imagination, & when I was 9 years old, a mental health professional, determined I needed conselling for stress I'd underwent during my parents divorce. This counselling halted the drawing I'd been doing in class of cartoons I loved on TV, & made me study. I wasn't born with a disability, but I was disabled by a counsellor, & when I was 18 they determined my drawings, (which I started again in school) needed to be stopped so they put me in the hospital, & gave me medication which I take to this day. Just like disabling the wheels on a chair to keep it from rolling, my mind was disabled to prevent artwork my mother, & the school thought was a problem. When I was 27 my friends, & I put out an album, & a year later, when I was 28, I was involved in a car accident, & thrown into prison. Convicted completely unfairly, & taught how to be a man by alcoholics working in the prison itself. Now, the jail had to have anticipated the entire year I sat in there before going to prison because, the 8,000 dollar debt I owe the jail to this day was the same the week I got there as it was the week I left, & being indigent the entire time, it should have started at a few dollars, & grown. Not have been predicted & submitted the day I got there. This is how I know, & I'm never paying them off.

CHAPTER II

FOR YEARS IN mental health, we were forced upon taking our medication. As much as we hated it, (as all medicine) we were force fed it. We were reminded, & given the meds in a routine untill we could finally stomach them, & could actually take them every day no matter how we felt about it. Now years later, I'm haveing to remind staff where I get mental health services to give me my meds, & if I forget, & haven't bus fare to pick them up before the end of the day, I don't take them that night. Now, normally in years past I wouldn't have minded & would have gladly not taken them. Of course, back then if I didn't take them I was hospitalized & put back on them. These days I am forced to ask for them & remember them as if (unspokenly) I won't get my weekly spending check if I quit taking them. I see this as a form of manipulation, & I thought manipulation was some sort of way to get what you want by using other means other than force on people & controlling their actions. A way used my the mentally ill & what mental health taught people not to do. So now, were being manipulated by the people who origionally taught us not to manipulate other people. Or has the world gone crazy? If there's one thing I know you shouldn't start a sentance 'or', so why aren't they sharing either?

CHAPTER 12

IF YOU MAKE the highest note possible, you can break glass without actually hitting it. If you die without telling your secrets, what can you achieve? I think Sid may have known who killed Nancy, & I think he was pretty obvious about it when he soluted whoever was interviewing him in The Exploited video I saw. In Brittian, the only people you'd swear a false alegance to would be Nazis, & I think The Nazis killed Sid Viscious, & Nancy Spongen. Probably while on heroin. I was looking for a place to live, & I got a random text from some people who were offering me an apartment anywhere in the USA. I thought it was a little wierd, so I told them to stop texting me by saying, "If you want to live, stop now". They said something like, "Oh, what 'rubbish' now I see your not serious". I thought it was wierd they used the word 'rubbish' in America. So, I called Johnny Rotten's fan mail line because, I thought he was in danger. See, He'd moved from England, & I'd been sending him fan mail. I thought if anyone was after his life, they'd have the Brittish lingo. You bet there's Nazis in England, & the same people that killed Sid, & Nancy might have very well been after John, & trying to go through me. The guy that answered the phone totally got it, & I apreciated that. "People who live in glass houses shouldn't throw stones", but if you can make the highest note possible at your moment of death, you can break every fucking window out of this place too, & very simply destroy the world.

A safety pin through the scrotem will help achieve that note, or you could just take The Pistols word for it.

CHAPTER 13

L ET'S TALK ABOUT 15 minutes of fame. Can you imagine going to many years of University to learn how to sing, & landing one line in a comercial. Thinking you're gonna get paid for the rest of your life doing this. So you write a book, & go on some late night comedy show. Then when you're asked if you sing, you say you don't even sing to your 2 year old kid. After that the comedian asks you about your book which is titled something about never stopping learning, (something from an old

TV comercial too from 1993) you comment about how your mentor told you to try as a musician. The comedian asks you if you did try, you lie & say you did. Then, to top it off you find out they only published one copy of your book, & you're the only one who read it. Several times I might add.

CHAPTER 14

“MUTUAL MASTURBATION SHOULD be taught in public schools.” “I second the motion” because, they showed us all those horrible pictures of STD's when we were 6th graders, why not teach the same age kids how to get off without making horrible mistakes that take up the next 17 years of their lives? Simple safe sex is unatainable because it's inconvienent to have to put on the condom, & abstinence is something most teens do not want to practice. Why not teach them how to have a hell of a lot of fun together without all the headache that comes along with being an adult? And then we get rid of this pesky abortion issue altogether now too. Pro lifers are really combatant, & Pro choicers, dismiss me as a drug dealer walking down the street. If they start teaching mutual masturbation the same time they teach about STD's then stress goes down among the young people, & I bet even gun violence if we learn how to love before it's too late. I don't know, I learned with girls, but I said whatever I could to get those damn Christians to back off & get off the sidewalk where I walk every day. The bus driver approves.

CHAPTER 15

SO, THE NORTH African White Rhino has gone extinct. The last male finally died. They had to put him down because his frail 45 year old body gave out. There are still two females left alive. Poachers hunted them to extinction, & you can't blame them. The amount of money they earned from one rhino is equal to 20 years wages. The scientists managed to save his sperm cells though. So, he's frozen in liquid nitrogen, & someday they may reintroduce white rhinos into the wild. Like some Jurassic Park story, only with mammals. Now, that is science. Leo the Gorrilla died too. These days extinction is being helped by old age among most endangered seniors.

CHAPTER 16

WHEN I WAS 15 1/2, I was in an auto accident with my mom in the passenger seat. We were sideswiped on a 50 mph road on the way to my work at the raspberry machine one summer. My mom was really mad at me, & blamed the whole crash on me. Even though she was the liscenced driver in the car. I did not want to get my liscence after that, & I didn't untill I was 17 when my mom stole my only $400 out of my bank account. She then paid for 4 mo. insurance on a pickup she bought for me to drive. I did not still want to drive. I used to kick dents in the truck, & eventually left it in a farmers field by the river. 10 years later, I was involved in a huge head on accident in another truck. A man was killed, & as soon as I woke up from the coma, I was arrested, & eventually convicted & sent to prison for Vehicular Homocide. The hospital pscychologist asked me right away, "Why did you do that?" & the lawyers kept on asking, "What was going through your mind before you crashed?" The explanation is that I was scared to drive, & never would have except my mom forced me to get my liscence when I was 17 after I quit driving by choice when I was 15 1/2. So, when I crashed my truck at 27, it was because I was afraid to drive the entire time, & was overwhelmed by traffic on Highway 20 like I've been saying all along. The system is flawed so people like me suffer, & so backward that while I was in the helocopter being airlifted to Harborview, the rescuers called it a, "Preemtive terrorist attack". Despite the fact that the pressure realease meant I had never felt that good & haven't since. You'd be surprised at how good altitude feels along with a few broken bones when you get away from your phobia for the first time ever. Another reason why I'll never drive again is simply the cost of maintaining a vehicle is unbelieveable, & they break down every other week. It's the stupidest thing on the planet. Plus the mechanics will fix your clutch, & then they go, "Well, the wheel berrings were worn. So, I tightened them up. Now, you better come back in 2 or 3 weeks cause they're gonna fall apart." So, you gotta work your ass off at a temp job, & loose more money the next month because your on SSI, & as soon as the wheel berrings are fixed, your valve cover gasgets need changing, & if you don't know what those are, it'll cost ya. Jello Biafra says they call that "Free Enterprise". It just means they want to rip you off. Driving is way over rated, & public transportation is safer, less expensive, & way more fun. Plus it's reliable, & you don't have to worry about assholes on the bus. Everybody I know on the bus is cool. All the assholes stay off the bus.

CHAPTER 17

UNIMPORTANTLY, THE THREAT if evil is high in this town. We have a witch living on the West side of our world famous Skagit River. I nick named her Negative Space due to her black complection. She used fly around the woods above my head when I was homeless & camping down there. At night, she would rub the back of my neck, & say, "Oh, you're such a good boy". I actually found her black kitten down there one day, & fed it. A year later, I was reading near a public bathroom, &

the kitten, (all grown up) came by & boxed me into a corner. I had to jump two fences to avoid crossing it's path which means seven years bad luck as you probably already know. Anyway, when I jumped the second fence in the dark, it was a 3 foot drop longer than I thought, & I really hurt my ankle. I went to the doctor, & he told me it wasn't broken twice. I still think it was due to the fact that I'm still feeling it a year later. There has been several aparitions I've seen too. Sometimes I see black figures out on the lawn when I look around. You blink, & they go away. I don't know what to make of it. Twice now, I've me cats that speak too. Is this a sign of witchcraft?

CHAPTER 18

HAVE YOU EVER thought about cruel & unusual punnishment? I have some for you. Jagged, cement, high powered, cold showers. Showers of these kind followed with no toilet paper unless you ask, but the availability of such toilet paper is not made known, & a green smok with 24 hour servelance cameras. This is what they call suicide watch in the mental health prison of Washington State. Now, Washington State is not Texas, & certainly not LA, or New York. So, this punnishment is definatly creative.

Cruel, & unusual kind of implys creative. The violence in such mental ward is astonishing, & idol hands was how one fellow inmate discribed our wait of four hours after a fight where a C-O was given a broken neck. Usually mental patients are surprisingly non violent, but in this ward, they were very violent, & over fed, & unhappy.

CHAPTER 19

ONE THING THAT I know is that I can-ada never become the president of the USA. Now, Trump on the other hand is upset with the fact that so many Mexicans are getting into the country now, & disapearing once there in here, & never coming to court for their citizenship hearings. This I find humorous because, out of fear, & the fact I stand out in a crowd, I went to all my court dates. I don't have the benifit of looking like the rest of my people to those in athority. I go to court to fall under it's mercy. Also, I find it humorous that Trump is failing to force Mexico to pay for the wall to keep more Mexicans from entering the country illigally. If at all we learn anything from Obamacare it's that in the USA, there is no dictatorship. So, in four years when a new leader is elected, (preferably) any law can be changed by the new people in office. When Trump leaves office, the new president might allow Mexico to pay to have the wall demolished, & give some of the Mexicans left in Mexico some legitimate work. Here in the US, funding for the Census is going up. Hard to count people like Cowboys, & Terrorists need a higher funded census beurou. Excuse me, military veterans, & migrant workers. But what are these Mexicans supposed to do? They have a currupt government in Mexico, so they seek the safety of the USA, & move North, & now our government is considering deploying the US Army to the US Mexico border to stop them from entering the country until this wall is built. Mexican people are now becoming the Cyrian citizens of the Western Hemisphere.

CHAPTER 20

NOW, WITH ALL the shootings in schools, malls, & in the work place we're not safe there. Plus drive by shootings keep us afraid in our homes. So, the USA is pretty much a very dangerous place to live if you don't have a gun, or is it? Well, if you have a gun you better be ready to use it, but if you don't then somebody who does that guns you down is essentially killing an unarmed man, & thereby in the wrong, but does this matter to modern day gun men? They say that having a gun in the house increases the chance of someone dying by gunshot wound in the house by 100%. The answer if obvious, don't buy a gun. Same goes for school teachers. If none of the teachers take weopons, less gun fights will occur in schools. You have a teacher with a gun, you have a dead kid, even if all the kid has is a dart gun, & gets taken wrong, she's dead. Don't arm the teachers, give them pay raises. Give them what they want, don't add to the violence. They've had security guards in schools in places like LA for years. That's fine, & those armed guards enforce safety, & so do the metal detectors because, any threat at school is defused at the door. Arming the teachers makes school an unhealthy learning envioronment, & is lethal for the country because when all the kids are in danger from both gun men or teachers, they don't care nothing about their school work, & the people behind the violence, the ones helping it catch on, the ones who want this to go on in public schools, achieve what they want. Nobody learing in public schools. So that religious people can control their women better, & that's the facts behind it. They want the kids ignorant.

CHAPTER 21

I TURN ON the news this morning & there was a woman who shot 3 people at YouTube in California. Overnight all the comercials were erased from all my favorite music on YouTube. No longer are there all these boring ads interupting Pennywise, & Bad Religion. What luck, & how great for the shooter. Now, even though she is deceaced, her death actually meant something. A lot more than any of the other shooters. This woman actually took a bite out of advertising.

She didn't kill anybody either. Except for herself, none of the 3 people she shot died. This is good news, no innocent victims. Just the change agent performing the deed needed to be done to remove the advertising. She was only pissed off because of sensorship anyway. Let's hear it for a pissed vigalanty who signifigantly reduced the advertising on YouTube.

CHAPTER 22

SINCE AFRICAN AMERICAN guys call each other brothers, & so do white guys, in relation are we all cousins? That's a good way to think about it, like if it is what it is, then it are what it are too.

CHAPTER 23

THE DEAD KENNEDYS have a song called "Chicken Shit Conformist". It's about how some people are really hardcore punk for like 6 monthes, or two years. Then all the sudden, they need a real job. Why all the sudden to they need a real job? Is it God? Do they worry deep in their soul that God doesn't want them going down the wrong path, & then they need to get a job & be just like their parents so they can be good Christians & give to the church? Probably so, I think because somebody really has to convice them of that. The Bill of Rights guaratee's us as Americans the right to religious freedom. This means there is no uniform church in this country. As you should probably know, rights aren't given, you have to stand up for them, & I think the right to being a non believer should be excercised. That's why I won't believe in God, & I hope I never will. There's a much more positive message being spoken by the youth, & the message of Christ is not new, & probably false. The message of Christ is too generally spoken over. People who are not good people, who use drugs or sex to get power over young people also spread the gospel, & that's how I know it's a fake message, & not very good. Drug dealers will literally bless the crystal meth before they give it too you. This is not a good thing.

CHAPTER 24

SOCIAL MEDIA HAS been blamed for the mass shootings of the last 20 years. Now, I know social media is bad. Not for egging on inverted teens, but for digging hooks into people, & demanding money out of unsuspecting kids with credit cards. I used to have a debit card, & in one or two nights I emptied my account & wound up almost 160 dollars in debt to Facebook. They had me managing a site & seeking buisness for my independent art company from Brazil. It's a total sham, & I'm still in debt to this day to Facebook, & I'm really trying to think of a way to pay off that bill. Not because I want to boost more posts, but because I hate being in debt. Buisness management is something I know absolutely nothing about, & I have no idea why anybody would think I ever did. Somebody thought I'd be able to understand how to sell my art on Facebook, & the minute they figured out I didn't have the money to pay anymore, & I wasn't knowlegable on how to scam people, Facebook stopped. Television, & YouTube have advertisments in various intravels to fund their programing. Facebook doesn't have any adverts. So, this leads me to believe that they sucker a lot of people besides me into boosting posts so their posts can reach more people. Leading people to think they're stars. When actually they are just being suckers.

CHAPTER 25

IT'S NO SURPRISE to me that there are so many homeless encampments showing up around the cities lately, there have been nomadic people all over the world since the dawn of time. These same peoples are now labeled as homeless, & athorities are trying to remove their encampments all the time. Nothing's changed it's just that these people are reverting back to their ancestors ways lately due to less jobs, & increased price of homes. Not to mention decreaced size, & land space. People start to revert back to the ways their ancestors lived when faith in God, & government fail. It's no change to them to be dirty, & sleep on the ground, in fact I think they rather it that way, & I don't think anything the government does can change that. I think until most the people in the cities die from some mass extinction, there won't be enough room for everybody, & the homeless are gonna occupy one way or another. These homeless, (nomadic) are far more creative at the ways they live, & cloned Nottingham Soldiers are gonna have a hell of a time irradicating them all. The Sherriff himself sitting in his stolen White House isn't gonna be able to get them off the streets that easy either, & although most of us do not like homelessness, some don't mind & prefer it that way, & these guys we used to call gypsies, aren't gonna die off anytime soon.

CHAPTER 26

A LOT OF other countries worry what will happen to them if they get sick while visiting the USA. Some Canadians actually buy insurance before they leave Canada & travel to the US just in case they get sick while visiting. They are that worried about the crazy price of health care down here. So most pray to Christ they never get sick here, buy God save you if you get in trouble. See, when they choose jurors in a criminal case, they pretty much choose people who have already decided you are guilty before they've heard the case at all. So, they've pretty much got you nailed if you decide to fight. That's why if you're charged with anything it's usually less time to take a plea bargain. Usually dragging it out in a court battle involves spending tax dollars, & they use the plea bargains as insentive to just give up, & do the time. Either way they're gonna win, & it's less trouble for the aristocracy if you just go quietly. There are way more people in prison in the USA than in any other country in the world. Is it because people don't know difference between right & wrong here? Probably not, in fact it's probably due to the fact that it's just a bad place to get in trouble. Not on the terms of currupt policemen stories in say Thailand, or Mexico, but in the USA. It's different here though, the cops will shoot you point blank & get a 3 day suspension with pay. That's as currupt as it gets. Not only this but in prison they oppress the inmates, (Offenders) using the worst form of oppression on the planet, Idol Hands. There's a fight? Everybody else sits in the chow hall together for the next 6 hours, & that's the way it is.

CHAPTER 27

NOWADAYS, SO MANY people are on food stamps there's nothing in the conveinence stores, but overpriced junk food cause that's quick & easy, & people get it free. That's why it keeps selling, it's free. I have foodstamps, & I buy food for my kitchen, but when I'm homeless, & I don't have kitchen, it's easy to buy food I can eat right now. That's what we have to get away from, the food for right now. The chips & the soda's & the candy. There's a conveinence store I shopped at today, & that's all there is in the store. All they have is the stuff for right now, & at that place it's not priced so bad but other places it is, & I fear a separation between people who pay cash, & people who use foodstamps is coming. How, & why are this; remodels turning regular convience stores into part time barbeque restaraunts. This means people with cash buy the hot food, & foodstamps pay for the junk food & the soda shoppers. Ever so slightly separating the rich from the poor. We've been told the rich get richer & the poor get poorer, & now I think I've found the seam. One goes up while the other goes down, & it's now just separating those with jobs from those without, & it isn't churches behind it, it's just those with jobs, like the ones that own the store, wanting something better. So, yea it isn't bad...

CHAPTER 28

ONE COULD SAY that since the democrats & republicans have been running against each other & ruling this country for such a long time back & forth that voting Green isn't a spoiler but more of a disagreement. You have the right to disagree, that's the freedom of speech. So, rather than voting democrat or repbublican, & falling in with the rest of the crown & being totally unheard, why not vote green, & disagree. That's your freedom of speech, the right to disagree. They say that if you don't vote either Democrat or Republican in the USA, your throwing your vote away. This is a total lie. If 95% of the country votes either Democrat or Republican, & 5% votes Greenn or Libertarian, then your vote goes a lot farther if you vote within that 5%. A drop in the bucket goes a lot farther than a drop in the Pacific Ocean. So, don't believe them if they say voting Green is a spoiler vote. In all actuallity, your vote actually does count more if you vote Green or Libertarian because so many less people vote that way.

CHAPTER 29

I RECENTLY SAW an interview with Gene Simmons from Kiss. He was being interviewed about new artists, & how most new artists weren't being paid for their work fairly. The interview was mostly about Spotify, & the new artists on Spotify. Whether or not Spotify was paying people for their work fairly or not. Now that spotify is selling stock & all. Gene Simmons did a wonderfull interview, but then halfway towards the end, he changes the subject mid sentance, & goes off on some rant, "I'm a straight guy, I've never held a joint in my life". Where he got onto that subject matter I'll never know, but it sure had nothing to do with Spotify, & the stock Spotify was selling, & had nothing to do with paying new artist fairly. My old band Diagnosed has an album on Spotify, but you can also find the album on YouTube, & listen to it free there. So, it doesn't really give anybody the initiative to buy the album on Spotify if they can listen to the whole thing on YouTube does it? For this reason, I believe since Gene Simmons got paid all his millions in the 70's for his albums, I don't think he has much to say about the digital wave of music these days. That's why we have to mix the old days with the new ways, & keep writing music & making art without it being on the internet. Getting people to come & look at your art or share your music on cassette or CD. Preventing the piracy & expressing yourself without some computer executive making a quick buck off you.

CHAPTER 30

DURING THE WTO riots of '99 or '00 my friend & I were carfully removed from society, & locked in captivity in a mental institution. We understood that the cops battling the protesters were so drug free, it was like they were on acid. We also thought it was a little strange we were in captivity at that very moment, & couldn't go to Seattle & participate. Personlly, I read the book years later, & found it strange that the whole thing was pretty much forgotten the minute it was over,

& I haven't heard a damn thing about this little battle on the news or any mainstream media since. Is that good or bad? Underground, it's been talked about consistently ever since, & people are quite happy about the way things went down. Will there ever be anything like that again? More than 10,000 protesters in Seattle at one time protesting Global Consumerism, & Corporate Feudalism. New Feudalism, & the corporations that do things like keep the Dolphin safe tuna labels on the cans of tuna in which gill nets are still used to catch the tuna, & dolphins are still being caught in. The WTO is not spoken of in main stream media, & people should be widly aware of what they do. Things like The Exon Valdese oil spill, that still effects the places in Alaska where the oil was spilled back in 1989, & hasn't gone away. Why don't we hear more about the WTO? Is it because these corporations are running the country & screwing the poloticians from behind? Leading every word they say to the public, & writing their scripts? I saw Donald Trump throw his script aside last week. It's good said John Lydon that Trump is exposing most of these corrupt politicians for what they are, & throwing them out of the government, but I do agree, a buisnessman in office isn't much better. Maybe john's right when he says, "Next we can get someone intelligent in office". Bill Gates says he could never have imagined how valuble computer software could have been when he was in school, & software was just what he liked to do. I find it hard to believe a plastic telephone can be as valuble or more as the last Da Vinci left in private hands which sold for 459 million dollars last year, but Bill Gates has made billions more off software. Which is, "Designed for the dump" I might add.

CHAPTER 31

I DON'T UNDERSTAND how people like that Gary Ridgeway can murder multiple hundreds of women, & none of the women get the better of him. He doesn't look that strong. I don't think I could take a lot of women. A lot of women could probably kick my ass. The mojority of them anyway. How did he do it, & how did drag the multiple hundreds of bodies off without throwing his back out. The guy wasn't that young. Most guys are a little tired & have aches & pains. How do guys like

Gary Ridgeway actually have the physical strength to carry out these cerial murders? Another thing is most the policemen have things like dogs. You find a body, (in water or not) & there's a scent a bloodhound can go find. Hundreds of women turning up in The Green River, & a blood hound could go find at least one of them. That's why I don't believe in this cerial killer myth.

CHAPTER 32

I N 2008, THIS country was sort of divided between those in power who wanted to keep on bombing Iraq, & Afganistan, & pretty much most the people who wanted to end the war. So, we elected president Obama, who ended up stopping the wars in Iraq, & Afghanistan, & gave us a new aproach to health care. The new aproach to health care has been stomped out & now we're looking at a nuclear war with those in the East. But I liked Obama, & he really did make it feel better here.

Only thing is, once he was elected, in the following 4 yerars. I went from a high rise apartment to a prison cell. Then spent the next 5 years working out of that. During the 2008 election, I was friends with a bunch of old guys in my apartment building. One of the old guys, was an old Beatnick. He made me promise never to join the military even if I need the money, no matter how bad it gets, Never. I really plan to keep this promise. To help get the Republicans out of office during this election, I used to read my poetry at a pub in the neighbourhood. My poetry has been lost, but some of it that isn't lost is other poetry which inspired mine. I'd like to share one poem that inspired me to write now.

DIE FOR OIL SUCKER by Jello Biafra

You! You look like you're just the ripe age to be drafted. Does that even bother you? Still thinking about that? There was a sign at Jones Town behind Jim Jones's dead body & it said, "Those who do not remember the past are condemned to repeat it". Those who do not remember the past are condemned to repeat it. Which would you rather sacrifice, your hot car or your life?

Die for oil sucker. Born on the fire cracker 4th of July, raised on football, & MTV, never felt what it's like to have to fight to stay free. Vietnam just a Time Life Book memory. The mask is off again, this time nobody cares, but you can't keep dancing when your legs are blown away. Die for oil sucker, sucker, sucker. You too can get your face shot off wo arms race tycoons won't have to get a real job. The cold war's over it was only a mirage. We could use that money we've got problems to solve, but we're not allowed a chance at The Peace Dividend cause our psycho president's got his head in the sand. Saddam Hussien so egocentric he even replaced Mickey Mouse on watches with his own face. Last Spring he was our tyrant, we thought we could use. We sold him his guns, & his nerve gas too. When he told our ambasador he was fixing to invade, April Glasgey told him, "No problem, Uncle Scam wouldn't care". What kind of a Bush league double cross is this? Cheap oil? The price has already gone up. This still could wind up making Hiroshima look like a picnic. Keep in mind James Baker is a born again Christian. Does he believe in Armageaden, & the last generation? Die for oil sucker, sucker, sucker. You too can get your spinal chord snapped. To save greedy kings from the greed of Iraq. Give your life for a country where women can't vote, & people still get their hands & heads chopped off. In Saudi Arabia they'll stone you to death, for sleeping with another persons husband or wife. Women can't go out alone, or show their face, or even drive, & there's never elections you can't even ask why. But they finally did outlaw slavery in 1962. So progress is being made, & they're sitting on something we can learn to live without. Certain fat cats bank accounts cannot, oil. For this, you get to be all you can be, a dead army, navy, airforce, marine. Come home one of those deranged unemployed vets. The kind they love to make TV cop shows about. Just like Tom Cruise in a wheel chair. No film royalties cause nobody cares, about you once you've been used to, Die for oil sucker, sucker, sucker. It'll kill the poor even faster than crack. Send them off to war, make sure they never comeback. Give them tanks that fall apart, & helocopters that crash. 2,000 die in Panama cause the stealth can't shoot straight. 800 million dollar Batman plane, & it doesn't even work. No surprise when their idea of national security is toilet seats costing 1,800 bucks, & is it really worth it in this day & age, to end up the winners of a world war three? Think about it, once we take over that place, we'll never ever ever be able to leave. Somehow we think we're gonna waltz right in. To colonize their hearts & minds. But the Arab people are now so damn mad. We'll be lucky to get out of there alive. You think any of them want their kings to sell us oil? Think of the cost to keep our army there. When the only way left to bleed oil out of the ground, is soldiers guns treating Arabs like slaves, or was that all part of the plan? Gotta put 400,000 NATO troops somewhere. They found a scam to extend the cold war. It's called, Die for oil sucker, sucker, sucker. Cause America The Beautifull is going to Hell, we no longer make cars or TV's very well. Our economy's rigged on selling guns & making war. What happens when no one wants our products anymore? America The Powerfull has hit a decline. Our cities & our people are falling apart. Malnutrition, & infant mortality rates to rival damn near any 3rd world slave state you name. Got one thing left to sell & that's the world police, a mercinary state to ensure there's no peace. We love doing your dirty work, but ya'll gotta pay. Mob style protection money to the US of A. Rich thugs with no vision trying to save their empires. New World Order mafia with them still in charge. Reducing America to a bannana republic. Die for oil sucker, sucker, sucker. What's so sick about this is there's a better way. Stop selling guns to Arabs & to Isreal. Don't need to keep ourselves hostage to oil. Use our Star Wars knowhow to build solar cars. (won't need an army either) One clerk in the pattent office might be all it would take, to find blueprints for a solar car General Motors shelved away, but oh no that's too simple, & there's money to be made. Especially if you already have more than you'll ever need. For those of us who can't buy our way out like rich folk like Dan Quail do, it's burn your draft card, burn the flag, & burn the pentagon too. That's why we got the worlds 1st tabloid war. No bodies, no funerals, no wounded, no gore. Super bowl every day where we always win. So much yellow ribbon we are hanging ourselves. That's what's so different from ugly Vietnam. Media that brought that war home's been bought out. General Electric controls NBC news. They want to sell weopons, they distort what we view. Can these Rah,

Rah, Rah, we love war poles be believed? When so many of us everywhere are out in the streets. Pentagon parrot papers won't admit we exist. What that says to me is their owners are scared. That we will get as strong as they have in Berlin, & tear down their walls, & their New Order scams. Yellow ribbon McCarthyism can't hold us too long. We support our troops most cause we say, "Bring them home". So be all you can be, say no to the army, navy, airforce, marines. Get off your butt before your butt's blown off. Don't die for oil, don't be a sucker!

I like this because since the recruiters came to my high school looking for kids like me for the military I've been against war the entire time. I quit all PE when signing up for my classes for my senior year, & took all my art classes required for graduating in 12th grade. I even skipped the graduation ceremony to avoid being seen by the real baby killers. The army recruiters that sucker kids right out of High School. When that old Beatnick made me promise to never join the military. That was like a dream come true.

CHAPTER 33

A COUPLE TIMES I've made friends on the street with girls. I just say "Hi" now & then. A couple times though I have seen these girls later, & they have their faces all scraped up. I don't know who does this to them, but they're definatly cowards. I'm pretty sure if I asked the girl what happened she'd say she fell, or have some sort of excuse, & wouldn't tell the truth. This girl we'll call Cindy, I had to work with in the kitchen at the homeless shelter here. I knew her boyfriend & he was a stand up guy. I made friends with both him & her. Now, last week while I waiting for a bus, she walked by, & her face was all scraped up & her eyes were black. All I have been doing differently is not buying drugs. One drug dealer though was pushing me trying to get money out of me. I told him no twice. How could that be linked to me? I don't know, but it seems like somebody was sending me a message when she walked by. I know she didn't do drugs, & neither did her boyfriend. He had a job, & they were working to get in an apartment. Last I heard she had a job too. Who would have scraped up her face? It's completely unlike her boyfriend, & know he didn't do it. None of the people we were friends with would do it either, & it probably had nothing to do with me, but I still feel to blame, & I want to help her boyfriend find who did it if he wants to find them. I know it's sort of stupid to wanna be a hero, but scraping up a girls face is definatly wrong. I think though, I probably have to catch this happening, & stop the fight while it's happening. Then I could really beat the guys down that are doing this to chicks. A lot of writers write about stopping war, & saving the environment, & skulls & stuff like that, but what about what is happening on the streets outside while we're all in bed sleeping. I guess the police are supposed to deal with all that, but in some neighbourhoods in LA, the cops won't even show up to calls.

There's a place in Bellingham, WA where the trails go through the woods where the cops won't even go there alone. I think the cops are out of control though, & they, as much as anyone else could be responsible for her face being all scraped up.

Cops have been shooting & killing guys regularly on the news since I've been watching lately now that I'm not homeless, & I don't think they really have anything keeping them in line. I got sucker punched & called the cops right away. Not because I was scared, but because I lost a tooth, & I figured this should be reported. They just said, "What do you want us to do?" & left me there. I then went to my step dads, (whome I detest) & beat his ass. I was stuck in court for a year & a half & got stuck with 5 years probation. I'm not going to the first probation meeting tomorrow. The same guy who sucker punched me, kicked me in front of witnesses a year later, & when I called the cops even though there was witnesses, it was so much trouble to actually get the guy charged I thought I better not & dropped the charges. This means my step dad went completely out of his way just to pin this assault on me when he very easily could have been a man & dropped the charges, & we could sit down & sort out the issues behind the fight. When I was charged with Vehicular Homocide, I was facing 29 years if I didn't accept a plea bargain. I took the plea bargain, but in this bout with my step dad I fought it, just to see, & they actually pick jurrors that already have decided to find you guilty before the trial starts. So, since I don't have assetts to protect me from violence, & I don't have assetts to allow me to be violent, these guys were able to beat me up & convict me for it. That's Nazi violence in your country my fellow Americans.

CHAPTER 34

WHEN I WAS in High School, like I mentioned before I was damned by my mother with that boulder, excuse me truck. Now, I had nobody to ride in the truck with me after I started hearing voices. One night they started trying to make me think, "If you're a man, you can kill yourself". I ended up in the ditch where a friend pulled me out. This friend later killed himself. Now, if the athorities are in charge of the voices like I actually believe & they were trying to make me think that if I were a man, I could kill myself, then they were very well putting words in my mouth during the vehicular homocide trial where I was supposedly crashing into cars to end my life, & they actually believe this, & are making young people who stand up for themselves the targets of their own violence. I think they wanna wipe us all out so they can have total control of the country that's why sagging your pants is gay etc. etc. Truth is they may be powerless if they don't stop us this way. At a local center I hang out at a lot the other day. I decided to go out for a smoke, but I walked around the building to pick up trash which I never normally do. When I went to throw the trash away, I saw the cops were walking into the building right where I should have passed. When the cop left a few minutes later he drove past me & nodded like a stereotypical insecure man, & I thought, "How strange, I have this probation meeting Monday, & they're trying to pull me in". The same people who made up all these lies about me wanting to kill myself, & put me in prison. Locked doors don't stop them, but can I? I know I didn't want to die!

CHAPTER 35

SID VISCIOUS DEFINATLY didn't kill his girlfriend Nancy Spongen. As you can tell by his note, he loved her. So, who did? I think it was the nazis.

Punk was primarily anti-racist. Notice the Swaztica he called punk. Was that cause he knew something perhaps? Speaking of musicians, they don't loose their hearing. When you learn to tell the different notes apart when playing a stringed instrament, it seems to change the way you hear normal sound. Most sound seems dulled, but you can actually hear the difference between different notes. So that part is fine tuned. A lot of people think you need earplugs at shows which I don't disagree with, but musicians don't experience hearing loss so much as a hearing change.

CHAPTER 36

THERE WERE CHEMICAL attacks in Syria on normal citizens again. I like the Syrian people because, they aren't with the Syrian rebels or the Syrian government. As troubling as it is to watch children dying, we don't want Putin & Russia attacking us over here. So it's best to just let them fight it out in that part of the world. We really don't need to be the world police, & Russia is strong, & Russia won't hesitate to attack the continental USA. I think Putin wants just as much as us for that violence to stop, but the US army can't do anything to help. They need to work it out themselves. Sending food & medical supplies to the people is one thing but military action is going too far. We should have learned from Iraq, & Afghanistan that we don't want to get involved in a war that the American people are fundamentally against. Not to mention the trouble it will bring from Russia if we get involved militarily. We don't need an attack over here, nope!

CHAPTER 37

THERE'S AN OLD joke that says, "You paint 1,000 pictures, & nobody calls you an artist, but you suck one cock". That's the problem, America hates artists. You can't get a wage like in Ireland for being a poet. In fact, most poets throughout history die penniless. Most people can only dream of making a solid living off art, & you pretty much have to be an art teacher, or a frammer to get paid with anything having to do with art, but everybody wants it. It's like the number 9. 9 is an even number, it's an odd square. It's alone like an artist, & the best art comes from the pits of depression & vulnerbility. To make money selling art, you need style, & technique. Most of the art students work in my class was essencially crazy, but I got an A, & I'm proud of that. I'm to the point where I'll pay taxes if I sell maybe one piece next year. Just you wait, wait & see. The government's already breathing down my neck. Any money I make off my art goes right back into my body. See, I always buy food & cigarettes with the money I make off my art, & it's always pretty small amounts. Like 20 to 80 dollars. Not much to worry about. I've yet to sell any paintings, & I'd declare any such income at or over what I'm allowed to make on my disabily check per month. 20 dollars is well below what I need to declare according to the rules of SSI, but 80 is the amount I'm allowed to make. So, at 80 I put that into my taxes. The government is taxing the hell out of regular citizens now. I was told a womans 1,800 dollar check went down to like 1,300 after taxes. That's gotten out of control. I have the benifit of a special needs trust which does my taxes for me & I can let them know if I make enough off something I want them to declare when they file taxes for the trust. So, I don't have to do it myself. Taxes are a bitch to figure out. That's how they got Al Capone, tax evasion. I guess I can learn from him, "I am like any other man, all I do is supply a demand".

CHAPTER 38

WATCHED A LITTLE of the Facebook debate. The rules are a document 1 1/2" thick. Nothing compared to ObamaCare, & basically Facebook is a low grade way to excercise your freedom of expression. There's nothing wrong with that. Unfortunatly, the government is stuck on Twitter, & want's to compete. They asked him if people signing up for Facebook have any, 'Earthly idea' what they're signing up for. I'd say probably morso than when signing up for the military. I saw on the news how to check if my information had been hacked into, & it had not. Bassically Cambridge is the government, & the government is now charging Facebook for a crime the government commited. Facebook are not 'data brokers', they did not sell any of the people's information, the government stole it. Facebook got jacked. Cambridge broke in, & stole, & you can't call government officials to put an end to government corruption. The government was seeking some sort of intelligence that does not exist, & all they're finding out is that we're friends. Bassically being whiney assholes. One such Senator who was cut short by time asked Mark Suckerberg, "What about Chinese Sensorship?" Chinese Sensorship is in China, & China is communist. Chinese Sensorship also is a regulation on the internet designed not to impose on their freedom of speech. Which is something that our government is trying to get Facebook to police. This is very wrong & our government is wrong to do it. If Cambridge is accused of mining Facebook users information, why isn't the law protecting Facebook? I think since they used the Facebook data during the Trump campaign, Trump probably used the info to do a 'Cross Check' when he stole the election. First he stole the information of young voters around the country, & then he deleted people with like names without them knowing. They proved this in the debate when one senator made a joke about how 'this morning I was told by all my friends there was another me on Facebook, & a picture of me posing with another senators family'. The senator was basically bragging how they got away with stealing the election by cross checking.

CHAPTER 39

I HAVE SEEN a lot of drinking straws all over the ground for a long time. Existencialy, I thought they were people trying to point at different things. On YouTube the other morning I was listening to music, & a comercial came on saying that the younger generation is 2 billion strong. Now, if the 2 billion young people all quit using drinking straws, it would signifigantly reduce ocean pollution. Later, I went to the store, & on the way out I saw another drinking straw on the ground. My normal thought that someone was pointing was changed to people litter those, & we need to quit using them. Existencialism is what I was told if fit into by that old beatnick. I thought I was an anarchist until he told me about existencialism, & that I was really an existencialist. Now I know because I changed something in my way of thinking to make me a better existencialist.

CHAPTER 40

OBVIOUSLY MR. TRUMP doesn't think with his brain. He's launching missiles at Syria. Russia is arming warships to protect their assets in Syria. In repsonse to the chemical attacks of course. Like I said, Russia warned the US to stay out of Syria, & I think Mr. Trump just wants to blow stuff up while he is in office, & doesn't want to leave office without blowing up some country with half our size & 1/10 our population. I bet he thinks we can take Russia if they want to fight us. He's definatly talking shit. Don't forget there's now 459 million USD in Russia after we bought that Leonardo last year. I thought that would be good for relations. Now, I think Russia's just like, "Thanks we needed the money, we'll use that". I've noticed the politicians tend to say, "I'll follow up with that later", & then the camera shuts off. Like there's stuff they don't want to say on camera. This means yes, they're keeping secrets, & have most likely been doing that all along as now, they're getting careless.

CHAPTER 41

WHAT'S ABSOLUTLY INSANE is that we smoked pot for years when it was illigal, & it took years to learn how to say no to the stuff so we could quit. Now, it's for everyone, & it's all over the news every day. People are finding all these things they can do with it, & politicians are going into the marijuana buisness. I sit back & laugh at all the hype over a drug I was taught was wrong, would lead to reproductive issues, & would lead to crime, & lying. You can see none of the people on the news are stoners. You can see all the kids out there buying the stuff don't know the feeling when it's illigal, & it's a crime to get stoned. It's really laughable, & the Washington State government is making a bundle off taxing the stuff. That's the main reason I don't smoke it anymore, the taxes. Not to mention I don't think it's the same thing as it was 25 years ago. I think there's new kinds of plants, & the high is different. It all changed for me in 1999 when I did acid. After that I didn't like pot any more, however it took 10 or 15 years to stop smoking it, & I had to go to coke, & speed to get high. That's right uppers were way better. Pot's a sedative like heroin, & therefore I can't handle it. These days the only drugs I do are the ones pescribed by a psychiatrist, & I like it that way. After completing drug treatment last year, I don't do drugs basically because the ones I like are illigal. I don't want to have to commit a crime to feel that way again. So, I'm just staying sober. Heroin is the most dangerous drug of all, & the penalties for being caught with it aren't as bad as speed or coke which aren't as bad for you. The rest of the downers are legal. Alcohol, & pot, however I just don't like the feeling I get from either, & I get the rush I need from a cigarette just as well. Being sort of in the know, I can get my roll your own tobacco tax free sometimes. As long as I'm willing to walk a mile.

CHAPTER 42

WELL, THE PRESIDENT launched the missiles folks. For a different reason then I thought though. He launched missies against the Syrian regime because the chemical weopons used on the Syrian people have been illigal since World War 1. This makes us the world police even more. Saying, "Maybe someday we can be friends with Russia, & Iran maybe not". I don't see him trying real hard. You know Russia really likes Canada, it's just they don't like America. According to the president, "America has a lot to offer". Well, we could also get bombed by Russia for trying to police the rest of the world, & I don't think the people of the USA are ready to defend themselves on their own soil, although most of us do own guns. It is good however to stop Syria from using chemical weopons. Because, they've been illigal since World War 1 the Brittish Prime Minister says we can't let it become normal for countries to use them all the time. I agree with her, & even though Putin swore our missiles would be shot down, I haven't heard that any of them were. This is the second time the president has shot missiles at Syria this term. The first time he wasn't supported by any other nations. This time England & France are supporting him. I think it saves them money to have the great & powerfull military of the US takle precision strikes against countries that commit war crimes against their own people. Whether or not the people of theat country call the strikes a farce or not.

CHAPTER 43

T HEY HAD SOME long talks about paying musicians fairly for their work. I think this is a good idea since my old band, Diagnosed has had an album out for 10 years, & none of us have seen any money from that at all. It's even on Spotify now. So, maybe if they start paying musicians fairly, we'll get some money.

CHAPTER 44

THE PRESIDENT ATTACKED the free press which is crucial to have in a democracy. Calling it fake news, & doing the exact opposite of what Jello would do which is DON'T HATE THE MEDIA, BECOME THE MEDIA. Maybe the press will get ahold of some good information like they did to expose Watergate. Then maybe (even though he's been exposing politicians) Trump will be exposed. Since he's been acting like he's above the law. One politician who Trump fired calls Trump a mob boss. I have always thought of him this way. I think He's only building the wall against Mexico to protect his friends in Vegas. When the president was addressing the country about the strikes in Syria, he mentioned how we in the US have the strongest economy in the history of the world. I thought Trump would be good for the economy when he was running. He's a buisnessman, & we anarchists are not fond of buisnessmen, "Buisnessmen are snakes that swim in streams of money". It gives me a different outlook on the rest of the country though, the country looks a little more mighty, & not like it's gonna fall apart like it seemed it were for so long under Bush & Obama. The president doesn't have the right to blow up somebody elses country. What if they did that over here? Right now, we've got 2,000 troops in Syria, & 6,000 on the border against Mexico. What the hell has Mexico done? & I wonder if Trump used the actual US army at all. Did he get Congress's aproval to declare war, or did he hire Haliburton to go blow up Syria without actually declaring war against Syria. I don't think war's been declared. The difference is, this time they struck targets where they knew chemical weopons were being made rather than blowing up a country & killing the leader. Then not finding any weopons of mass destruction. No civilian casualties, but no word on whether war was declared either. It's a contradiction, the people of Syria support the government of Syria. Why would he use chemical weopons on them when He's winning the war against the rebels? That's what the people are asking, & the government of our alis don't believe it was the rebels because, the chemicals were delivered by way of helicopter of which the rebels supposedly don't have. Helicopters are flown by the government but not the rebels. So our alis assumed it was the government of Syria. The people of Syria now are protesting the US bombing.

CHAPTER 45

APERENTLY WE'RE NOT staying in Syria. Just a quick vulger display of aggression, & pull the troops out right away. To stop Syria from using chemical weopons that have been illigal in warfare since World War 1. Now, they're saying that Russia is backing off too. I don't think Putin's giving in to this little strike. The people of Syria called it a farce. Russia see's this as a move in Chess. Now they sit back & think about their next move. Remember Russia has been fighting wars a lot longer than Trump,

& knows a thousand years worth of history in warfare that Trump, (a business man) doesn't know at all. I have a feeling Russia is thinking, & that's is something Nazi Trumps are known to not do. Look at this little strike. How much thought went into that? Not that much, it was planned & executed in a matter of two days. We still don't know what kind of fire power Putin's got under his power, & we won't know until he does something with it. Mr. Trump, 'when you least expect it, expect it'. From the look on Putins face in some camera on TV, he's taking this very seriously, & Trump is a go getter, money maker who knows very little about Chess I'm guessing.

CHAPTER 46

WE HAVE NEW alis in the Middle East, which is weird. We had to completely eliminate the ones in power & set up governments that we liked. This way, the people there are ruled by leaders friendly to us. Problem is, it's a little transparent. There's no substance to these puppet governments backed & armed by us. The Saudi's have always been in power. It's the same royal family there that hired us to get Saddam Husein out of Kuwait over Osama Bin Ladin, though now have gotten rid of

Hussein, the new Iraqi government isn't quite feared by Iraqi's so if we take our eye off them for even a moment. Boom, violence erupts. We'll never be able to leave. The new Saudi prince isn't quite such a lovable western fellow either, & the more money we pour into his country for his oil, the bigger the risk we take of him hiring foot soldiers to come back at us. And the new generation of kids in those countries will be taught by people who remember the war, & they might not be taught to be friendly to Americans in the Middle East. The New World Order is bassically The West taking over the world, & they had to start in The Middle East. Cause that's where the oil is that we need to fuel The War Machine. And now, Trump is starting shit with Russia, I don't think Russia is gonna stand for it. The minute we cross the line. The minute we infringe on Russian rights. The minute we go into Russia with a gun, we're under fire.

CHAPTER 47

YOU KNOW, BULLYING can drive some kids to suicide. How do we know the perpetrators of all these school shootings aren't the victims themselves? There could be a man behind the mask, metaphorically speaking. There could be somebody tormenting these kids into killing large amounts of peers, & then killing themselves because there's no other way out. Sometimes in prison, there's sexual abuse, & the only way out is to call the Pria hotline on the telephone. I got called into

Pria because, some guys were making fun of a guy with a pacemaker, & he almost died in prison. The pria people wanted to talk to me, & I told them the reason the old guy was probably acting weird was probably his pacemaker. When I got back to the unit, the biggest bully told me not to talk to Pria again. I never had to. There could be some underlying issues within the school districts making kids lash out in violence & suicide. Feeling it's the only answer out of desperation. How many people actually want to kill a bunch of people & then kill themselves, & we don't get to interview the shooters because they're all dead. So it keeps happening. When I got to recieving in prison, they made us watch a video on what to do if you find a candy bar on your pillow in prison. Apperently that's some kind of inuendo. Most of us would just pick up the candy bar & wave it in the air screaming, "Thank You!" it's so stupid it's not even funny, & the cops in recieving said not to tell, they'd rather catch the guys. So, let's just wait & see, & keep the doors locked at night to prevent any candy bar depositors from dropping in.

CHAPTER 48

IT'S NOT A witch hunt! Kurt Cobain was probably murdered. Why do I agree with this theory? Because, people lie about stuff like that. My Grandfather supposedly died of a self inflicted gunshot wound too, & when I went to his house, there was no blood anywhere. There was no sign anyone had been shot anywhere, & to this day people who think Kurt Cobain wasn't suicidal say there was no blood where he died either. His Grandfather said, "There were no prints on the gun, not even Kurts". If this is true,

& there were no blood stains either, then he did not kill himself. We just have to wait & see if the photo's of Kurts death scene are released. He was to have done a lot of heroin too, & typically, why do we use drugs? I know I did to fill one void. The fact there wasn't a woman in my life. Heroin, Speed, they all simulate one thing, "Love & Sex". Kurt Cobain had a wife though, so did Sid Viscious have a girlfriend. Sid died becase the one he loved was murdered. Kurt was supposedly pained by the rockstar life. Seems strange he would do that since as artists we make art hoping it's sucessfull. Could it be they were both, one & all the victims of bullying? I was walking down the street, & I saw a kid with his Tuba case. I yelled, "It's the band geek mafia". The kid took off running accross the street. He followed the traffic laws, & pushed the buttons to cross the street correctly though. So, maybe that was what happened in my car accident too. Maybe they were just out to get me because I was in a band. Maybe Sid, & Kurt too. Maybe they were victims of people who wanted to hurt them for playing music, & being nerds. Don't forget, my grandfather, the one who supposedly shot himself as well at 86 years old. He was a violin player, so.

CHAPTER 49

T HEY DISCOVERED AN enzyme in a Chinese landfill that eats plastic. This is good now the garbage will finally decompose. There has to be an evolution link in there somewhere. A few years ago we didn't have this enzyme, & now one's evolved maybe. I think evoulution happens when evoulution is nesiccary. So, it was nesiccary for this enzyme to evolve to eat all the plastic in the landfills & it has. This is great, & great for the environment. When we were second graders on Lopez Is. we were told that it can take as long a 300 years for a plastic disposable lunch tray to decompose. You could bury a paper one next to a plastic one, & 50 years dig them both up, & there would be little bits of paper next to a brand new plastic tray that you could wash & use the next day. So this new discovery of an enzyme that eats plastic is very pleasing to me. There's so much plastic in the world. In the oceans floating around creating dead zones, underneath the lawns, & in pretty much everything we use. To have something evolve that actually eats the stuff is very promising, & gives me hope. Moreso that The Bible ever could. Christians have a way of saying if they just believe, everything will be OK. It's not like that in science. Science has now found a solution to our pollution problems in a landfill in China. Yes, everything will be OK for the planet, & it evolved in nature. No god came to Earth to claim his kingdom, an enzyme evolved to eat something that was never going away.

CHAPTER 50

THE NORTH KOREAN leader has finnished testing his nuclear arsenal. On the news everybody was so happy because, He's not testing anymore. I think this is very grave news. Yes, he is not testing anymore. No, we're not safe because, he's armed to the teeth with tested nuclear missiles ready to launch. President Trump is now planning on visiting North Korea. If the Koreans don't want all of us to take care of the Earth as we've made it, what to stop them from cutting Trumps throat at dinner, & nuking a leaderless USA? We'll see, I could be wrong but that's what I'd do if I were North Korea. First I'd get China, & Japan on my side secretly. Then I'd murder Trump on live TV, & nuke the now powerless USA. Like a prime evil killer, revenge for Hiroshima, & Nagasaki. Or maybe they'll fall in love over dinner. Jello Biafra called the wars in Iraq & Afganistan a, "Short term orgy of violence". Maybe the two people with the most violent repituars at their disposal will have a short term orgy of impotence. The strikes in Syria were sure short & pointless. Though yes chemical weopons are illegal in warfare, why aren't nuclear weopons?

CHAPTER 51

HOMELESS CURTESY IS exagerated by the homeless themselves far too much. Now even people are going out of their way to hand homeless people 10 dollar bills out of nowhere. The homeless still go & buy booze, or smokes are what I bought. It is good to give, but don't give more than you can afford to keep eating yourself. I was homeless for quite sometime, but since I'm disabled as well, I had some income. I rarely bummed money for any other reason than to learn how to do it.

At times, when I was bumming money, people would show up out of nowhere & hand me free money. That was cool, but I just went & bought a pack of smokes. When people bought me food I liked that. Then I had a great meal & didn't have to pay for it. The programs for housing are nice, but I still don't trust everybody. Mostly because I have been in mental institutions since the age of 18, & I learned to hustle when bumming was forbiden. You have to sell extra smokes to buy yourself more, & the same goes for coffee. That's why I don't blame drug dealers. If they're making money to buy more drugs, & keep it going. Fat Mike from NoFx has a song called DRUGS ARE GOOD. They really are, & people over do it. There is such a thing as too much of a good thing. Like in SCARFACE, He just goes overboard on the coke in the end, & that's what does everybody in. That's what's doing the churches in, & the government. They're over doing it. I think nuclear weopons are overdoing it after the end of WW2, we haven't used them again. If we forget the horror, & mass killing that they're capable of, we could repeat that history.

CHAPTER 52

SO I STOOD in front of Planned Parenthood for 20 minutes with a sign that said, "Meat Is Murder". Nobody even honked once. It was fun though, & I did make a lot of people smile. I guess that's what it's all about, having fun & making people smile. One guy looked at me & went, "Yeah". This other guy accross the street with a stroller made me say, "Animals are for petting", three times, & finally as I was walking off the mound, a lady walking past me went, "Crunk". I think her head popped.

I just wanna be remembered like The New York Dolls. They went into jock bars dressed in womens clothing & went home with the jocks girlfriends. I like the way they did things so, standing in front of Planned Parenthood while the Christians who say, "Pray to end Abortion" aren't there with my sign that says, "Meat is Murder" was something I just had to do. I used to do things like that to show how stupid things I didn't like were all the time when I was a kid. Now, I just did it again, damn.

CHAPTER 53

I REMEBER BACK in '99 I started listening to the dead keneddys. I really liked PLASTIC SURGERY DISASTERS. I remember after I graduated, I kinda lost my mind. Not really, but everybody I knew at that time either had never heard them or didn't pay as close attention as I did. Maybe it's cause I started writing my own poetry. I don't know but I did start having a weak condition. First it was like my heart was beating out of my chest, & later when I was in the hospital for mental conditions, I got so weak I could barely sit up. Now, I have written quite a bit more, & I noticed the same condition in my friend Leo. He thinks he has conjestive heart failure & he's so weak he can barely sit up. He's fighting it though just like I did. I think the fact that he's fighting it, & he's getting through it is a result of the book I wrote that he read. Literature that puts you in the hospital, literally.

CHAPTER 54

POOR BILL COSBY was found guilty on 3 counts of sexual assault. The old dude lost his son 20 years ago, & now in his 80's is getting 30 years in prison. Some people put guilty signs on his hollywood star in hollywood. The women he alegedly abused are very overwhelmed by emotion, & he probably did have sex with them. At the time they probably saw nothing wrong, & then TV put a thought in their head that they could bust ol Bill. Bill Cosby plans to appeal, but don't most of the people found guilty in the modern fencepost justice system. I don't see this as the right verdict knowing what I know, & having been through a few trials myself. Again, they pick jurrors who have pretty much decided your guilty before they're picked to be on the jury. Any jurrors who might actually find you not guilty are removed during jury selection. What are we gonna do without America's Dad. Our token father figure for the pepsi generation is now a convicted sex offender. How rude of him, he called the prosecuter an asshole when they tried to take away his million dollar bail. Come to think about it, Donald Trump is a rich white buisnessman, & Bill Cosby is a rich black entertainer. They both have historys with lots of different women. Could it be Bill Cosby is only being held accountable because of his race, or ethnic background? Seems like it, the prosecuting attorney in his case is white. He's a "rich powerfull man", was he busted because he's black? Nobody on the news has said anything like that, but that's not because it isn't true, it's cause they're scared to say it, or they want to act like it isn't true. I see a serious race issue in this country. These artifact children are being raised racist in the 21st century.

We were taught in school that racism had to stop, & the civil rights movement came close to ending racism for our generation. Obviously some of the kids in our classes didn't get it because, they've raised thier children to be ignorant assholes, & carry on a tradition we were told was close to being dead. Racism is back & we need to bury it again. A lot if not all of these school shootings are being executed by white kids. I wouldn't doubt the kids getting shot aren't of minorities. Most of the teachers that taught my generation the holocost did happen, & so did the civil rights movement are getting old & retiring & these kids in my classes who secretly didn't believe it are getting teaching jobs possibly, & edjucation is being manipulated. They're probably thinking there's nothing people like me can do to change how they teach kids in elementary school, but isn't that why Bill Cosby was on Sesame Street? To change all that? Rock & Roll is one way I can do it. Poetry, prose too. Along with art, telling it like it is in my books. Bill Cosby plans to apeal, I hope he wins because, the Donald Trumps of the world just gain power if Bill Cosby is really convicted. We can start helping Bill Cosby by getting an African American man to be the prosecuter in the case of his appeal. Somebody honest. I noticed the prosecuter lied in my last assault conviction saying that I don't do the right thing. I'm a Canadian farm boy. I always do the right thing, & I really given somebody the shirt off my back. So that prosecuter lied in court to get a conviction & my city slicker public deffender had no disagreement.

So that would help & although we know politicians & lawyers are almost always dishonest my grandfather was an honest lawyer. So, I know they do exist. People jump to conclusions when somebody is charged with a crime, & assume guilt before the trial. Mostly the lawyers & the jurors. This leaves you unhappy in court which makes you even appear even more guilty. Plus jail clothes, or tattos etc. etc. Assuming guilt is the opposite of what the constitution says, & therefore wrong in this country. Most acuratly depicted in the Saturday Night Live movie, NOTHING BUT TROUBLE with Dan Ackroid, & John Candy. I'm not condoning sexual assault, but even though a good actor, I don't think Bill Cosby is the type of dude to do that. The judge is related to the bailif, who's related to the prosecuter, who's related to the & so on & so on...

CHAPTER 55

OVER NIGHT LAST night, Korea ended the Korean war. The leaders from both the North, & the South shook hands & made up. Our president is very proud. This means there won't be any nuclear threat from North Korea. This is best because we're not gonna destroy the world. We all take care of it. My friend Cher is a Korean. Him & I are pretty good friends. He runs a convienence mart here in our town. I do my best to be friendly for forighn relations. Back 20 years ago, my two friends used to steal cigarettes fron Cher. They would ask what the prices were way above his wifes head, & then when her back was turned grab a pack of smokes. We were 16, & I didn't like this at the time. Now they've become my friends. Two winters ago, I tried to do the same thing my friends did with a lighter, but Cher saw me before I could put it in my pocket. Obviously he learned how to watch his store better. He forgave me last week though. Just in time for North & South Korea to make up. Now, the president says when he goes to North Korea to make sure they're denuclearized, if he can't make peace, it's gonna be a tough time for Korea, & a lot of other countries. I sure hope not because, we don't need a WW3. The president has most of the west on his side though, & I fear that he will try to get the west to gang up on Korea, & their alys. I also fear he's underestimating the power of the east. Countries like China have Billions of people to fight with. So do countries like; India, Russia, & Syria. The west has a definate dillusion that we have the best military in the world & we may be mistaken because, we don't know for sure what the east has to offer militarily. That's why I'm afraid of Trumps grandure. The Koreans of course are afraid their country will be tricked? This I can see, & how? They like to flip a bitch, so your wrong either way. I can name an example, "You are either with us, or against us". That's what they said to me, & I said, "I am not with you or against you". I said this because, my belief is that I don't want to try to get people on my side & team up with me, I want to give them something. Rather than start a gang, I'd give an old friend a copy of his favorite punk rock album from my collection. This way we make friends & we're stronger than any army. I don't like the with us or against us idea because, if I choose to be with the Republicrats, I have to deal with their teasing & initiations. If I choose not to, I get to be killed by them. Someone like me looses. So, I choose the alternative, I'm the kind of guy who can't really work or go to school. I hang out in the art store. That's where I belong, & where I feel comfortable to call my home.

Yes, I think it's over. You can close the book now

www.ingramcontent.com/pod-product-compliance
Lightning Source LLC
Chambersburg PA
CBHW051105250726
48656CB00001B/486